modern
Parties

modern
Parties

Martha Gill

Photographs — Brad Newton
Chef — Shaun Doty
Text — Matthew De Galan

LONGSTREET
Atlanta, Georgia

Published by LONGSTREET PRESS, INC.

A subsidiary of Cox Newspapers, a subsidiary of Cox Enterprises, Inc.

2140 Newmarket Parkway, Suite 122, Marietta, GA 30067

Printed in Hong Kong by Paramount Printing

1st printing 1998

Library of Congress Catalog Card Number: 98-066362

ISBN: 1-56352-492-9

Digital film prep and imaging by Advertising Technologies, Inc., Atlanta, Georgia

Book design by Martha Gill and Vivian Mize

FOR JACQUIE GATLING,
PARTY ON!

CONTENTS

Introduction *xi*

modern
Parties

PARTY TIME – Wrapped in a pink and orange kimono, I stood in the doorway of my Florida home, waiting eagerly for my guests to arrive. I was four, and it was my first real birthday party. Once everyone was accounted for, my mother engaged us in the ultimate party game, pin the tail on the donkey. We played hide-and-seek in the sunny backyard and musical chairs in the living room, then ate chocolate cake with white frosting and strawberry ice cream. My friends left with bright smiles on their faces and candy-filled bags dangling from their

THERE'S ALWAYS THE CHANCE THAT SOMETHING WONDERFUL MIGHT HAPPEN

arms. As soon as they were gone, I had a realization: *I loved parties.* ✿ As I grew up, this love affair with parties only intensified. Even today, as a busy mother and career woman, I still get that age-old feeling of excitement at the thought of hosting a get-together. I enjoy having friends over and seeing people relaxed yet excited by the evening. At a party, there's always an element of anticipation, the chance that something wonderful might happen. To me, parties should be nothing more complicated than good food and drink and the company of people you most like to spend time with. ✿ But, the fact is, life *is* complicated. A few obstacles do stand in the way of hosting a party, modern or otherwise. ✿ Today we're all busy with families, careers and trying to stay healthy. Finding the time

and energy to entertain can be tough. Creating the right kind of party can be even more elusive. Over the years,

I've hosted a lot of parties, and I've often found that the less I did, the better the results. By this I don't mean serving

chips and beer. A good party requires thought and creativity. And, of course, some real work—hopefully fun work.

But the point is, don't overdo it. Having everything

"just so" is, well, just so boring. Think simple and

> I'VE OFTEN FOUND THAT
> THE LESS I DID,
> THE BETTER THE RESULTS

spontaneous. Let your own ideas rule the day. ✿ What does this mean in practical terms? What food and

drinks do you serve? How do you decorate? How do you make your party an occasion you and your guests will

really enjoy? These are the questions I try to answer in this book. And I believe you'll find some light and fresh

solutions. My goal is to help you have more fun when you entertain. That, after all, is why you should throw a party

in the first place. ✿ In the art of hosting, like so much else, I learned first from my parents. My

father is a professor at the University of Florida, and when I was a child he served as faculty advisor

to the student group that brought speakers to campus. Our house became the standard

reception site for an eclectic stream of renowned visitors—Margaret Mead,

Tom Wolfe, Abbey Hoffman, Coretta Scott King and Arthur Ashe, to name a few—as well as students and faculty members clamoring for a precious moment to chat over cocktails with a verifiable celebrity. My parents became very adept at this complex task, creating a relaxed and welcoming environment that put everybody at ease. When I wasn't sneaking a drink, I was watching and learning. You can pick up a lot watching a host deal with, say, G. Gordon Liddy (no jokes about plumbing) or Joan Baez (remember that her guru is a vegan). Over the years I put what I learned to use and discovered some useful tactics of my own. ✿ For twelve years I owned a design firm that specialized in creating images for large corporations. Especially in the beginning, I often entertained. I soon came

to realize that each party was a way to define my own image—for myself and my clients. I strove for

STRIVE FOR A CHIC AND EFFORTLESS TONE

a chic and effortless tone. And with two rambunctious children in the house, I needed ideas that were beyond the ordinary, yet still were simple and practical. As I learned to incorporate these ideas into my personal entertaining, I found that this casually elegant quality put our friends at ease and created memorable evenings that didn't leave me stressed, drained and wondering if I would ever throw a party again. I like my guests to feel pampered, but I don't want to kill myself in the process. If I'm still picking up toys or setting up the bar when people arrive, I try to remain calm, enlist help and enjoy. Really, what else can you do—not let them in? Remember, the point is to keep it simple, and plan just a little in advance. This book can show you how and, I hope, inspire you not just to have a party, but to savor the experience more fully. ❀ *Modern Parties* includes recipes created by Shaun Doty, the executive chef at Mumbo Jumbo in Atlanta. Shaun and his colleagues at this very modern restaurant

WE ALSO ACKNOWLEDGE THE NEED TO INDULGE A BIT FROM TIME TO TIME

share with me the philosophy that great food is all about preparing the simplest, freshest ingredients with spectacular results—a hand-rolled pasta with sweet butter, garden sage and freshly grated Parmesan, for instance, is far better than an elaborate lasagna with eighteen packaged ingredients. The culinary style that pleases scores of Mumbo Jumbo patrons works very well when entertaining at home, where the goal is to create dishes that inspire the palate, but don't overwhelm the cook. Modern doesn't mean slaving and stressing in the kitchen. But it does

mean enjoying the tactile and sensory delights of cooking—and even more, it means eating well. *Modern Parties* tries to find a sensible middle ground

between enjoying the best foods and living a healthy lifestyle. Many of the dishes we offer in the book are as healthy as they are delicious—consider, for example, our vegetarian dinner featuring purple Thai rice with chickpeas and bok choy. But we also acknowledge, and fully endorse, the need to indulge a bit from time to time. Today we all want the best tastes, the best drinks, the best every-thing. And why not? Life is short. We deserve a slice not only of the good life, but of the best life. Still, we also want to feel good and stay healthy. I've always believed in moderate indulgence. My solution, therefore, is to go ahead and enjoy great tastes like farmhouse cheeses, foie gras, cigars and chocolates. But not all

WE ALL DESERVE A SLICE
NOT ONLY OF THE GOOD LIFE,
BUT OF THE BEST LIFE

at once, in the same evening. And not in imposing quantities. Pick one and make it the focus of your party, surrounding it with lighter and healthier accompaniments. I believe this philosophy of moderation does more than leave you feeling better at the end of the evening. It also helps you to appreciate and pay attention to what you are eating. Focusing on one or two tastes gives you the time to really enjoy your food instead of having the palate overwhelmed with different flavors. ✿ But food is only one part of the party story. *Modern Parties* also includes advice on decorating, cigars, cocktails and other tips to help you play the good host. You'll learn to

create floral arrangements from whatever happens to be in your garden or on your kitchen windowsill. Select

cookware that's equally at home in the kitchen or in

a formal dining room. Create tablesettings that are

PREPARE SIMPLE, FRESH INGREDIENTS WITH SPECTACULAR RESULTS

original and spontaneous, like stacked newspapers for a brunch buffet. Mix up trend-setting cocktails, like our

multi-hued Martinis, and select the best spirits and wines for themed drink parties. ✿ We've

divided the book into four sections that flow like the course of the evening itself. The

suggestions in "Cocktail Parties" can help you start off a dinner party or serve as stream-

lined cocktail party fare. We sought out quick recipes and show-stopping flavors, like tuna tartar

and foie gras. "Dinner Parties & Buffets" includes recipes for main courses, side dishes and desserts.

These range from the elegant (roasted quail) to the retro/down-home (short ribs with macaroni

and cheese). "Parties" provides food, drink and random hip tips to make a gathering memorable.

"Into the Night" delves into the sweet haze of digestifs, desserts and after-dinner smokes. We offer

some tips and insights on the current cigar craze to help you get started if you want to light up your life. Finally, you'll find an extensive Resource Guide that will help you locate specialty foods and hard-to-find items.

As you use this book, remember that no party will be — or needs to be — perfect. Parties are full of priceless moments, and their planning and preparation should be too. So put on some music, pour a glass of wine, pull out your cutting board and start chopping. It works for me. I hope it brings you the same joy.

Enjoy your party! — *Martha Gill*

Beautiful to look at, beautiful to eat. Tuna tartar is a close cousin to sushi.

Tuna Tartar

A N D   C H I L L E D   S A K E

TOKYO COCKTAIL HOUR – So much of what we regard as modern has its roots in Asia, and especially Japan. Clean lines. Organic shapes. Colors and textures derived from nature. An esthetic that measures beauty by its harmony with the natural world. This is the Zen we seek with our tuna tartar and sake. It's the perfect combination for an early evening cocktail party or a light tasting before dinner. Both food and drink are light and clean and won't overwhelm the palate or spoil the appetite. We surround them with an eclectic mix of decorative elements: a decanter with a raffia "necklace," wooden placemats and sushi blocks, origami paper, a homemade oil lamp. The goal is to emulate for your guests the chic neon bustle of a Tokyo bistro. The tuna should be exceedingly fresh, but don't let this intimidate you. Nearly every city has a good source for sushi-quality tuna these days. You should also find some 2-inch ring molds (available at some kitchenware and hardware stores) to shape the chopped tuna and give the table a flash of drama. A few notes on sake: In Japan, sake is a passion akin to the French passion for wine. Sake tasters have some ninety unique words to describe different subtleties of flavor. Sake is becoming more and more popular among Americans, who especially like it cold. Yes, this is acceptable. The taste is piquant and refreshing. And serving it cold means no fights with the microwave. Try a few varieties and make a high ritual of the tasting.

IMMERSE YOURSELF IN
A DISTANT NIGHTLIFE

1

SAKE

- Junami Ginjo Sanka, Masum
- Tokubetsu Junmai, Oyama
- Jumai Daiginjo, Wakatake Onikoroshi

TUNA TARTAR

Chef's note: Ring molds in various sizes are available at many kitchenware shops. The molds are not essential, but you'll need them to make the most dramatic presentation.

- 1 ¹/2 pounds tuna, brilliant red in color with firm flesh
- 2 tomatoes, peeled and seeded
- 4 shallots, finely minced
- ¹/4 cup finely chopped chives
- ¹/4 cup finely chopped roasted peanuts
- 2 tablespoons peanut oil
- Salt and pepper
- 1 (1 pint) container alfalfa sprouts

 Good sources for Asian tableware and decorative touches include the Japanese department store, Takashimaya, and Fellisimo (see Resource Guide).

Carefully dice the tuna with a sharp knife into $^1/_8$-inch dice. Transfer the diced tuna into a stainless steel bowl set over ice. Dice the tomatoes into a size equal to the diced tuna. Combine the tuna, tomatoes, shallots, chives, peanuts, and peanut oil in a mixing bowl. Season to taste with salt and freshly cracked black pepper.

Using a 2-inch ring, mold the tuna tartar onto the center of individual plates. Be sure to pack it tightly into the mold so that it will retain its shape when unmolded. Remove the molds and garnish with alfalfa sprouts. Serve with toasted baguette slices or something crispy to act as a counterpoint to the tuna.

Serves 12

How to serve a single malt? Generally, straight up or on the rocks. Some enthusiasts believe a little spring water loosens up the whiskey. Others vehemently disagree. In any case, no soda or other mixers.

Foie Gras

THE RICH ARE VERY DIFFERENT – Yes, the rich are different. They have more money, as Hemingway noted to Fitzgerald in their famous exchange. Thus they can afford, in theory, limitless supplies of the very best diversions, from a Bentley in the drive to a butler at the door. Plenty of the rich choose instead to live in ranch homes, drive late-model cars and indulge in nothing more exciting than ranch dip and Budweiser. But that's the realm of reality. We prefer to cling to an elegant illusion, a glamorous mythology of wealth in which Fred and Ginger dance in grand hotels and on the decks of ocean liners. And in this pantheon two minor but important deities are single-malt Scotch whisky and foie gras. The very best of each is fabulously expensive and decadently satisfying. They are the perfect cornerstones for grand celebrations or quiet moments in front of the fire on a winter day. The combination is also a marvelous preamble to a steak dinner or a night at the theater. Foie gras, a terrine of duck liver, hails originally from Gascony, the renowned culinary region in southwest France. But as with so many other fine foods of European origin, American producers are now making superb domestic equivalents. The foie gras shown here is stuffed into "French Kiss" prunes. This sublime combination creates a rich, velvety, sensual taste. Single-malt Scotch continues to grow in popularity in America and worldwide. Made only in Scotland, single malts are generally smokier, heavier and richer than blended Scotch. Hundreds of brands are on the market, with evocative names such as Inchmurrin, Cragganmore, Macallan and Glenmorangie. Before you invest in a bottle, you may wish to sample a few varieties at a well-stocked bar. We've included some of our favorites here.

SIPPING THE GOOD LIFE, ON THE ROCKS

SINGLE-MALT SCOTCH

- Inchmurrin, 28 years old
- Macallan, 18 years old
- Oban, 14 years old

FOIE GRAS-STUFFED PRUNES

Armagnac-marinated prunes stuffed with mousse of foie gras are known as "French Kisses" at specialty purveyor D'Artagnan. D'Artagnan provides fresh foie gras to top chefs around the country (call 800/327-8246) and can deliver your order overnight if necessary.

 Party Tunes: Yes, he was a dancer, and the greatest one ever at that. But Fred Astaire could also sing—not flawlessly, but with style, charm and perfect phrasing. As Irving Berlin said, "His heart was in a song before his feet took over."

The multi-hues are the message in these modern Martinis.

Martinis

TAKE FIVE – It is the age of modern Martinis. You see them everywhere. Bright, beautiful and wickedly delicious. Mixed with passion at the most soigné lounges. Held aloft by the most elegant hands. Happily, the old debate over how much (or rather, how little) vermouth should corrupt the gin or vodka has ended. Instead, today we talk of color. The azure of the Mediterranean off Majorca. The smoky black of dusk in Buenos Aires. The pallid melon green found in certain Italian frescoes faded with the centuries. There is a vivid rainbow to choose from, with a corresponding spectrum of tastes. Here we offer a palette of five modern Martinis. The base is still vodka (substitute gin if you wish). But instead of adding vermouth and an olive, we turn to assorted additions ranging from cranberry juice to Black Sambuca. We leave the olives out of the drink and serve them as a light accoutrement. Use an assortment of olives and marinate them in herbs for a special touch. These modern Martinis are just the species of cocktail to embolden your will and loosen your limbs before a heavy round of hard-boiled swing dancing. Like the Martini, the music of Artie Shaw, Count Basie, Benny Goodman and a host of modern swing bands has carved out a place for itself in today's pop culture. The drink and the dance are perfect companions. Both speak of carefree sophistication and style, of romance bound up in the sway of music and the twinkle of color. Take five and try a bit of each.

A BRAVE NEW LOOK FOR THE KING OF COCKTAILS

ASIAN ORANGE MARTINI

- 2 ounces vodka
- $1/2$ ounce triple sec
- $1/2$ ounce orange juice
- Orange slice

Stir vodka, triple sec, and orange juice in a pitcher filled with ice cubes. Strain into a chilled Martini glass. Garnish with orange slice.

BLUE MOON MARTINI

- 2 ounces vodka
- $1/2$ ounce pineapple juice
- $1/2$ ounce Blue Curaçao
- Orange slice

Stir vodka, pineapple juice, and Blue Curaçao in a pitcher filled with ice cubes. Strain into a chilled Martini glass. Garnish with orange slice.

 Party tunes: Part swing, part lounge, mostly a genre unto its own, *Pink Martini* is perfectly named to serve as the soundtrack to your next cocktail party.

Black Opal Martini

- 2 ounces vodka
- 1 ounce Black Sambuca
- 2 to 3 coffee beans

Stir vodka and Black Sambuca in a pitcher filled with ice cubes. Strain into a chilled Martini glass. Garnish with coffee beans.

Woo Woo Martini

- 2 ounces vodka
- 1/2 ounce peach Schnapps
- Splash cranberry juice

Stir vodka, peach schnapps, and a splash of cranberry juice in a pitcher filled with ice cubes. Strain into a chilled Martini glass.

Wai Lin Martini

- 2 ounces vodka
- 1 ounce Midori

Stir vodka and Midori in a pitcher filled with ice cubes. Strain into a chilled Martini glass.

Don't mean a thing if you don't offer green.

MARINATED OLIVES

- 4 cups assorted high-quality olives, such as Cerignola, Niçoise, and Kalamata
- $1/4$ cup extra-virgin olive oil
- $1/2$ cup fennel fronds, washed and dried
- Freshly cracked black pepper to taste

Mix all ingredients in a bowl and cover with plastic wrap. Allow to marinate for at least 2 hours before serving.

Serves 12

This glassware twirls.

Party tips: Have a few pitchers of water on hand to give guests between tastings. And plan a post-tasting activity —maybe some tango?

Tequila Tasting

TEQUILA NACÍON – Tequila. Party. There is a kinship there. It's as old as the Aztecs and as recent as your last Margarita. But like all relationships, time brings changes. Today tequila means a very fine, very sophisticated spirit worthy of careful savoring and animated debate. Invest in a few bottles and make the evening a grand tasting, with the tequilas as the star. Tastings are a great way to bring people together and get them talking. And nothing induces speech like tequila. Parties like this one can take on a life of their own, so be prepared. You may start off carefully introducing each tequila and end up a small voice amid the hip and happy chatter. But that, in the end, is the whole point. So chill. Some notes on premium tequila: It is distilled from the heart of the blue agave plant, which looks like a cactus but is actually a cousin to the lily. Most tequila that is shipped to the United States is blended with other distilled spirits. Tough and brutal, this blend winds up in millions of Margaritas and shot glasses, producing an ocean of giddiness and innumerable hangovers. But a very small amount remains unblended. This pure blue agave spirit is bottled in and around the northern Mexico town of Tequila. (Distilled agave made outside of Tequila is called mezcal, and there are many excellent producers.) Fine tequila comes in three basic varieties: *Blancos* or *Silvers* are bottled immediately; *reposados* (literally, "rested") are aged two to six months in oak casks; *añejos* are aged more than one year. A good añejo compares favorably to Cognac and single-malt Scotch in its complexity and depth of flavor. To accompany your tequila journey, we suggest an avocado salad, vegetable crudités and boiled shrimp with a spicy South American sauce. Have some friends over early to help chop vegetables. Serve with olive oil—what could be easier?

THE MODERN MYSTIQUE
OF TEQUILA

TEQUILA TASTING
AVOCADO AND CILANTRO SALAD
SHRIMP WITH SOUTH AMERICAN COCKTAIL SAUCE
RAW VEGETABLE CRUDITÉS WITH E.V. OLIVE OIL

TEQUILA

BLANCO/SILVER (FRESHLY MADE)–

- Porfidio
- Chinaco

REPOSADO (AGED 2 TO 6 MONTHS)–

- Zafarrancho
- El Tesoro

AÑEJO (AGED OVER 1 YEAR)–

- Barrique
- Gran Centenario

AVOCADO AND CILANTRO SALAD

- 8 Haas avocados, ripened until just soft to the touch
- 2 red onions, finely diced
- 2 tomatoes, peeled, seeded, and diced
- 1/4 cup chopped fresh cilantro
- 1/4 cup extra-virgin olive oil
- Juice of 3 lemons
- Grilled pita wedges

Look for the designation NOM (Norma Oficial Mexicana) to ensure the tequila meets the highest standards. Some famous fine tequila houses are Herradura, Porfidio, Jose Cuervo and Patron.

Peel, pit, and dice the avocados and transfer them to a mixing bowl. Add the red onions, tomatoes, cilantro, extra-virgin olive oil, and lemon juice. Season with salt and freshly cracked black pepper. Mix until just combined. Serve with grilled pita wedges.

Serves 10-12

SHRIMP WITH SOUTH AMERICAN COCKTAIL SAUCE

Chef's note: For ease of preparation, purchase already boiled shrimp.

- $^1/_4$ cup finely chopped red bell pepper
- $^1/_4$ cup finely chopped green bell pepper
- $^1/_4$ cup finely chopped red onion
- 1 tablespoon finely chopped garlic
- $^1/_4$ cup minced cilantro leaves
- 1 jalepeño, seeded and finely chopped
- 1 teaspoon cumin
- 1 teaspoon paprika
- 1 teaspoon white pepper
- 1 teaspoon chili powder
- 1 cup ketchup
- 1 tablespoon horseradish
- 2 tablespoons lemon juice
- Salt
- 1 $^1/_2$ pounds boiled, peeled shrimp

This glassware hails from a Kentucky flea market. Hunt for small, tequila taste-size glasses at antique malls, estate sales and auction sites on the Web (see Resource Guide for best flea market sites).

Combine all ingredients except shrimp. Place cocktail sauce in a chilled bowl and arrange shrimp decoratively around the rim.

Serves 10 to 12

VEGETABLE CRUDITÉS WITH EXTRA-VIRGIN OLIVE OIL

Use any combination of the following (allow 1 cup of vegetables per person):

- Red bell peppers, cut into 1-inch strips
- Green bell peppers, cut into 1-inch strips
- Fava beans, shelled and peeled
- Scallions, washed, roots and tops removed
- Endive leaves
- Carrots, peeled, halved, and each half quartered
- Fennel bulb, split, cored, and cut into 1/2-inch strips
- Celery stalks, halved and each half quartered
- Black radishes, skins scrubbed and cut into 1/2-inch sticks
  (Scrubbed whole red radishes can be substituted)
- Beets, peeled and cut into 1/8-inch rounds
- Extra-virgin olive oil

To serve: Arrange prepared vegetables on a serving platter. Pour olive oil into a separate bowl and serve together.

Herb Albert and The Tijuana Brass could dig it. Can you?

Market Dinner

A FRESH TAKE – Kick off those chunky black platforms. It's warm outside. Time to go barefoot and see how your garden grows. Time to connect with the sun and some friends. Time to dash to the farmers market and pick up something red and green and moist and fresh. No season lasts forever, so go with it. Case in point: tomatoes. Many of us like to have a few plants in the backyard, along with some basil and a few herbs. But if you can't deal with the dirt, definitely buy locally grown organic summer tomatoes. They're fresher, sweeter, richer—and the next best thing to growing them yourself. Here, we serve the tomatoes in a salad with buffalo milk mozzarella and basil. Simple, fresh and perfect. The whole roasted fish in our menu is easier than you think. If you're used to grilling fillets, don't let the head and bones scare you off. The bones make it less likely for the fish to become overcooked— so they're doing their bit. Above all, make sure that the fish is fresh. Look for shiny and firm flesh that springs back at your touch. Putting the fish in individual Le Creuset casseroles is our preferred method of cooking and serving, but our recipe offers an alternative method if you don't have the casseroles on hand.

TAKE A WALK ON THE FRESH SIDE

1995 Sancerre Lucien Crochet
Sauvignon Blanc, Loire Valley, France

Buffalo Milk Mozzarella and
Vine-Ripened Tomato Salad with Basil

Whole Roasted Fish
Tropical Fruit Granita

Buffalo Milk Mozzarella and Vine-Ripened Tomato Salad with Basil

Chef's note: Locally grown organic summer tomatoes are absolutely the best to serve, but very good quality tomatoes can be had as early as April (coming from Florida) and as late as September (coming from New England).

- 2 (6 ounce) balls of buffalo milk mozzarella
- 1/2 cup balsamic vinegar
- 4 vine-ripened tomatoes, cored
- 1/4 cup extra-virgin olive oil
- 1/4 cup basil, julienned

Slice each mozzarella ball into 4 slices and chill. In a small saucepan boil the balsamic vinegar until it is reduced to 1/3 cup. Allow to cool. Slice each tomato crosswise into 6 slices. Season with salt and pepper. Stack the tomato and mozzarella alternately on individual plates. Drizzle the olive oil and reduced balsamic vinegar around each plate. Scatter the basil over the top.

Serves 4

 Contact the Biodynamic Farming and Gardening Association at 800/516-7797 to locate the nearest Community Supported Agriculture (CSA) farm source, and enjoy nature's bounty through the growing season.

WHOLE ROASTED FISH

Chef's note: This dish is quite simple to prepare, as fish roasted on the bone is difficult to overcook. When shopping, seek out the freshest whole fish you can find. Look for shiny and firm flesh that springs back to the touch, brightly colored gills and no odor.

- 4 (1 to 1½ pound) whole fish such as pompano, striped bass, or red snapper, scaled, gutted and trimmed of all fins and gills
- Salt and pepper
- 1 bunch thyme
- 1 bunch rosemary
- ½ cup extra-virgin olive oil
- 1 tablespoon butter
- 12 peeled Italian cioppolini onions or spring onions, with tops and tails removed
- Lemon wedges

Preheat oven to 450°. Soak the whole fish in iced water for 30 minutes to remove any traces of blood. Pat dry. Season the cavity and exterior of each fish with salt and freshly cracked black pepper. Place each fish in an individual 11-inch Au Gratin Le Creuset casserole. Stuff each fish cavity with thyme and rosemary and drizzle 2 tablespoons olive oil over the fish. Place the casseroles in the oven and bake for 20 minutes. While the fish is in the oven, melt butter in an ovenproof sauté pan, season with salt and pepper, and lightly brown the onions.

Le Creuset casseroles are functional as well as beautiful. Place a trivet at each placesetting and you can serve the fish directly from the pans.

Place the pan in the oven and roast the onions alongside the fish, turning the onions once or twice during cooking time.

To serve: Remove the fish and onions from the oven. Divide the roasted onions among the casseroles. Garnish with lemon wedges and serve immediately.

Note: You can substitute for the casserole dishes a baking pan lined with foil and sprayed with nonstick cooking spray. When fish are cooked transfer to individual oven heated entree plates.

Serves 4

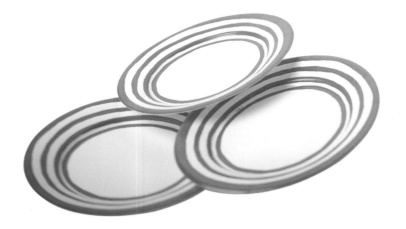

Surprise! These hip spiral plates are made of paper.

TROPICAL FRUIT GRANITA

- $3/4$ cup water
- $1/3$ cup sugar
- 2 cups passion fruit-orange juice (about 20 passion fruit and 1 cup fresh orange juice)
- $11/2$ cups pineapple chunks
- $1/3$ cup champagne
- $1/4$ cup white rum
- Fresh mint leaves

To make a simple syrup, bring the water and sugar to a boil and boil for 2 minutes. Remove from the heat and cool. Hold the passion fruit over a strainer set over a bowl, cut the fruit, and scoop out the flesh and seeds into the strainer. In $1/4$-cup increments, pour orange juice over the seeds and press the fruit juice through the strainer to obtain a total volume of 2 cups. In a blender or food processor, puree the pineapple with the simple syrup and strain into a bowl. Add the passion fruit-orange juice, champagne, and white rum. Pour mixture into a baking dish that will evenly distribute the liquid to a depth of $1/2$ inch. Freeze for at least 6 hours.

To serve: Drag a fork over the surface of the frozen granita to create ice crystals. Spoon mixture into chilled dessert glasses, garnish with fresh mint leaves, and serve at once.

Serves 4

 Tropical fruit granita is a thirst-quenching cross between cocktail and dessert.

Purple Thai rice with chickpeas and bok choy is a delicious, healthy and stylish alternative to a meat-centered meal.

Veggie Dinner

ALL THINGS ORGANIC – Healthy can be hip. A dinner party needn't mean a night of excess. Nor should it be devoid of the sensual pleasure of good food. Happily, there is a way to have it all. Organic foods and inventive vegetarian cuisine are fixtures in many people's daily lives. Why not take it to the next logical level and entertain in the same healthy way? This is the world you can create for your guests with our Asian-inspired vegetarian dinner party. The centerpiece is purple Thai rice with chickpeas and bok choy, preceded by a sunflower sprout and daikon radish salad and followed by an easy, delicious tropical fruit soup. The striking blend of colors in these dishes will make this meal a beautiful sight on your table. A key tenant of modern is finding new and pleasing uses

A SOJOURN
INTO HEALTHY HARMONY

for everyday objects. Here we use wheat grass, all the rage as a nibbling garden for pets, as a centerpiece that evokes the natural themes of the dinner. Line up three to five wheatgrass trays in a row for an understated table setting that harmonizes with the themes of the meal. Many of the serving pieces for our dinner party are reproductions from mid-20th century designers, whose dream was to bring affordable, eclectic design within everyone's reach. Designers such as Enzo Mari and Eva Ziesel created strikingly original pieces that were beautiful in form and efficient in function. This is, in a sense, the same organic spirit we strive for with our vegetarian dinner. Have fun. Stay healthy. Two modern tenets of life that *can* coexist.

SPARKLING WATER
SUNFLOWER SPROUT AND DAIKON RADISH SALAD
WITH MIRIN VINAIGRETTE

PURPLE THAI RICE WITH CHICKPEAS AND BOK CHOY
TROPICAL FRUIT SOUP

SUNFLOWER SPROUT AND DAIKON RADISH SALAD

- 1 pound daikon radish (about 1 to 2 whole daikon),
  peeled and finely sliced
- 2 (1 pint) containers sunflower sprouts
- 1 recipe Mirin Vinaigrette

Combine sprouts and daikon in a mixing bowl. Gently mix with
Mirin Vinaigrette and serve immediately.

Serves 6 to 8

 Eva Ziesel was a pioneer in designing functional, organic ceramic pieces for mass production.
This vase, designed in the 1950s, is available again from the Museum of Modern Art in New York.

Mirin Vinaigrette

Chef's note: Mirin is a sweet and sour condiment found at Asian markets and some supermarkets.

- 2 tablespoons Mirin
- Juice of $^1/_2$ lemon
- $^1/_4$ cup peanut oil
- Salt and pepper

Mix Mirin and lemon juice. Whisk in peanut oil and season with salt and freshly ground black pepper.

Serves 8

PURPLE THAI RICE WITH CHICKPEAS AND BOK CHOY

- 1$^1/_2$ cups dried chickpeas (3 cups canned chickpeas in their juice can be substituted)
- 2 tablespoons curry powder
- $^1/_2$ cup peanut oil
- 4 cups purple Thai rice*
- Salt and pepper
- 4 tablespoons butter
- 8 heads baby bok choy

available in Asian markets and some supermarkets

 Arne Jacobsen designed this sleek, modern Danish flatware.

The night before: Completely cover the chickpeas with water and soak overnight. Mix the curry powder with the peanut oil to thoroughly combine. Place in an airtight container. The next day: Drain the chickpeas and cook them in fresh, boiling water for 30 to 45 minutes, or until tender.

Remove from the heat and keep warm in their cooking liquid. Cook the Thai rice in boiling salted water for 20 minutes, or until cooked but still firm to the tooth. Drain rice, add salt and freshly ground black pepper to taste, and toss with half of the butter. Keep warm. Split the bok choy heads in half and wash several times to remove all sand and grit. Blanch in boiling, salted water until tender. Drain. Place the remaining butter in a large sauté pan over medium heat. Add bok choy and sauté gently until well coated in butter. Do not brown.

To serve: Divide the rice among preheated serving plates. Top each plate with warm chickpeas and 2 bok choy halves and drizzle with 1 tablespoon of curry oil.

Serves 8

Party Tunes: Jazz pianist Keith Jarret's ethereal *Köln Concert* will help strike the right chord.

TROPICAL FRUIT SOUP

- 1 vanilla bean
- 1 quart white wine
- 1 cup sugar
- 6 whole black peppercorns
- 2 cinnamon sticks
- 1 mango, peeled and sliced
- 1 pineapple, peeled, cored, and sliced into chunks
- 1 starfruit, sliced crosswise
- 1 papaya, peeled, seeded, and sliced
- 2 kiwi, peeled and sliced crosswise

FRESH FRUIT MAKES
A STRIKING
AND DELICIOUS SOUP

Split the vanilla bean lengthwise and scrape out the pulp and small seeds. Combine the vanilla bean and its pulp with the wine, sugar, peppercorns, and cinnamon sticks in a medium saucepan. Bring to a boil and simmer for 3 minutes. Remove from heat and let steep for 10 minutes. Strain the soup and chill.

Ladle 1/2 cup of the soup into individual chilled bowls. Garnish each bowl with mango, pineapple, starfruit, papaya, and kiwi.

Serves 8

Heavy desserts don't suit modern lifestyles. You can satisfy the urge for something sweet with a fruit soup.

Vintage '50s plates, housewares and assorted tchotchkes help set the retro mood.

Fifties Dinner

THE NOSTALGIA OF FLAVORS PAST— Somewhere, in everyone's past, there is a place of comfort. A place that smells like Sunday roast dinner, sounds like Patsy Cline and greets us like the face of Betty Crocker, smiling warmly from a 1950s cookbook. It's just the sort of nostalgic destination to bring your friends to for the evening. Provided, of course, you update the past just enough so it's not passé. The goal is to strike a chord of comfort and warmth, with just a touch of playful irreverence—down-home, with a healthy jigger of downtown. To set the tone, head for the flea market or thrift store and pick up some retro plates and glassware. Then,

INDULGE IN SOME
COMFORT FOOD
WITH A MODERN EDGE

focus on the food. For this decidedly modern sojourn back to the 1950s, we offer new variations on a classic American dinner. Maytag Blue cheese and almonds breathe a contemporary, sophisticated life into green bean salad. Roast quail, topped with a fried quail's egg, sits atop hearty North Georgia grits. To finish, we offer Jell-O™, that most American of all dishes. Our recipe replaces the little pink marshmallows and fluffy layers of Cool Whip with such modern ingredients as flavored vodka and wild berries. You will be amazed—and inspired, perhaps, by the remembrance of meals past. Only this time around, they'll taste better.

1994 Nichols Pinot Noir,
Sierra Madre Vineyard, California

Green Bean Salad with
Maytag Blue Cheese and Almonds

Whole Roasted Quail with
Logan Turnpike Grits

Wild Berry Jell-O

GREEN BEAN SALAD WITH MAYTAG BLUE CHEESE AND ALMONDS

- 1 1/2 pounds green beans, tipped and tailed
- 1 cup Maytag Blue cheese,* crumbled
- 1/2 cup toasted sliced almonds
- 1/4 cup chopped shallots
- 1/4 cup peeled and diced tomatoes
- 2 tablespoons chopped chives
- 1/4 cup grapeseed oil
- 3 tablespoons sherry vinegar
- Salt and pepper

* see Resource Guide

Blanch beans in boiling salted water until crisp-tender. Drain. In a large bowl combine beans with remaining ingredients and toss.

Serves 8

 Stone-ground grits, which preserve the flavor and nutritional value of the grain, take longer to cook—and are worth every minute.

- 1 tablespoon butter
- 1 yellow onion, diced
- $1/2$ cup chopped ham, such as Kentucky or Virginia
- 1 pound collard greens, washed, stemmed, and julienned
- $1/4$ cup water
- Pepper vinegar
- Salt and pepper
- $1/4$ cup toasted pine nuts
- 16 partially deboned quail
- 1 tablespoon olive oil
- 8 quail eggs
- 1 recipe Logan Turnpike Grits

Place butter in a tall pot and turn the heat to high. When butter is melted, add onion and ham. Cook until onions are translucent. Add the collard greens and cook until they are wilted. Add the water, reduce the heat, and cook, covered, over low heat for 30 minutes. Add salt, pepper, and pepper vinegar to taste. Remove from heat and chill in a bowl.

Preheat oven to 450°. Combine the collard greens with the pine nuts and generously stuff the quail. Brush the quail with olive oil and season with salt and pepper. Place quail on baking sheets and roast for 15 minutes.

 Party Tunes: "Crazy." "I Fall to Pieces." "Walking after Midnight." Such sad songs, yet so strangely comforting. This is the legacy of Patsy Cline.

Brush a nonstick pan with olive oil and heat over low heat. Fry the quail eggs until the whites are set and the yolks are still runny (sunny side up).

To assemble dish: Divide the grits equally among warmed plates and top each portion with 2 cooked quail. Garnish each plate with a fried quail egg and serve immediately.

Serves 8

LOGAN TURNPIKE GRITS

- 3 cups water
- 1 cup Logan Turnpike Grits*
- 1/4 cup cream
- Salt and white pepper

* see Resource Guide

In a large stockpot, bring water to a boil. Add grits slowly in a steady stream, whisking until smooth and free of lumps. Return to a boil, then reduce heat to a simmer. Cook, whisking often to prevent lumps and scorching, for at least 30 minutes. The grits will be ready when they are of pudding-like consistency and are no longer crunchy. Remove from heat, add cream, and season with salt and white pepper.

Serves 8

Party Tip: Disasters happen. If your dinner hits an iceberg, take it in stride. Have a drink. Call for take out.

Chef's note: Wild berries can be found at some gourmet markets and roadside stands. Substitute cultivated berries if wild ones are unavailable.

- 1 cup water
- 1 cup sugar
- Zest of 1 lemon
- Zest of 1 lime
- Zest of 1 orange
- 1 (6 ounce) package sparkling white grape Jell-O
- ¼ cup Absolut Currant Vodka
- 1 cup wild berries, such as blueberries, raspberries, currants, strawberries, or any combination of these

WHEN WAS THE LAST TIME YOU HAD JELL-O?

Pour 1 cup of water, sugar, and citrus zest in a saucepan and bring to a boil. Reduce heat and simmer for 3 minutes, cool and refrigerate. Prepare Jell-O according to package instructions, using sparkling water, and add vodka. Place berries into 8 individual molds or 1 large mold and pour gelatin mixture over top. Refrigerate for at least 4 hours, or until set. Unmold Jell-O onto a platter or individual plates and drizzle reserved sugar/citrus mixture around Jell-O.

Serves 8

 Betty Said It: "Dessert! It's the high point of the meal. It's your chance to go dramatic, to be a little daring, to show you've been around."—from *Betty Crocker's New Picture Cookbook*, 1958.

Serve everything out of stainless steel storage containers for easy clean up.

Weekend Buffet

HARVEST MOON, INDIAN SUMMER – The days are shorter and cooler, and green gives way to red and brown. The light is sharper, clearer. And everywhere there is more bustle, more life, more urgency, as the last mild days before winter call out to be savored. It is autumn, and people rake leaves, sweep patios and listen to football on backyard radios. Families and friends visit, bringing appetites that grow larger with the changing season. This is the time to reach into the mythic American past for inspiration. Here, we've come up with a hearty buffet featuring braised short ribs and macaroni and cheese. It's perfect fare for a family get-together, a football party or a harvest moon celebration. Everything is prepared indoors, but can easily be served outside if there isn't too much snap in the air. As always, we advise simplicity. Julienne the vegetables for the cabbage slaw ahead of time and pour on the dressing just before serving. Use your stovetop as a food station to keep the short ribs warm and forget the hassle of a chafing dish. Keep desserts and drinks basic — brownies from your favorite bakery, some autumnal microbrews and maybe a few bottles of zinfandel. To decorate your table, set out on an impromptu fall foliage hunt around the neighborhood (children will love to help). Scatter a few of the prettiest findings on the table for a beautiful, unstudied look. Fashion colorful napkin rings with beads threaded onto picture wire.

SET OFF ON
AN AUTUMN ADVENTURE

45

1996 Rabbit Ridge Zinfandel (Barrel Cuveé)
Macaroni and Cheese
Hot Cabbage and Bacon Slaw
Braised Short Ribs
Brownies (from the Bakery)

MACARONI AND CHEESE

- 2 1/2 tablespoons butter
- 2 1/2 tablespoons flour
- 1 quart hot milk
- 1 teaspoon grated nutmeg
- 1 pound uncooked macaroni or other short-shape pasta
- 1 cup grated gruyère cheese

Make a béchamel sauce: In a large saucepan melt the butter over medium heat. Add the flour and cook for 3 minutes, stirring constantly, until roux is blond in color. Using a whisk, gradually add the milk and whisk until all lumps are gone. Add the nutmeg and season to taste with salt and pepper. Cook for 10 minutes over low heat, stirring occasionally. Remove from heat and cool. Preheat oven to 450°. Cook the macaroni in boiling salted water until cooked through. Drain. Mix the macaroni with the béchamel. Place the mixture in a buttered 4-quart casserole and top with gruyère cheese. Bake for 15 minutes, or until golden.

Serves 12

HOT CABBAGE AND BACON SLAW

- 1 head red cabbage
- 1/2 head green cabbage
- 4 carrots, peeled
- 3 red onions
- 3/4 pound diced bacon
- 1/3 cup red wine vinegar
- 3 tablespoons sugar
- Salt and pepper

Using a mandoline, cut all of the vegetables into julienne, or grate vegetables on the large holes of a cheese grater. Combine vegetables in a large bowl.

Cook the bacon in a sauté pan over medium heat until crispy. Pour the bacon and its fat over the cut vegetables. Off the heat carefully add the vinegar to the pan and return pan to the heat. Quickly bring vinegar to a boil and pour over the vegetables. Add the sugar and season to taste with salt and freshly cracked black pepper. Toss well and serve.

Serves 12

 Create a whimsical vase for the buffet with a handful of marbles and a glass of water.

BRAISED SHORT RIBS

- $1/2$ cup peanut oil
- 1 garlic clove, peeled
- 12 pounds short ribs, cut into 1-inch segments by your butcher
- Salt and pepper
- 2 $1/2$ cups flour
- 2 onions, coarsely chopped
- 2 carrots, coarsely chopped
- 2 celery stalks, coarsely chopped
- 1 leek, white part only, washed and chopped
- 2 bottles red wine
- 2 quarts unsalted chicken broth
- 2 sprigs rosemary
- 2 sprigs thyme
- 3 bay leaves
- 3 tomatoes, peeled, seeded, and chopped

Preheat oven to 350°. Season the ribs with salt and pepper. Place flour into a baking dish and dredge the ribs in flour. Pat off the excess. Working in batches, sauté ribs in a large deep sauté pan over high heat, in about 2 tablespoons of peanut oil until well browned on all sides, adding more peanut oil as needed. If pan becomes too hot, reduce heat to medium. Transfer ribs as they are browned to a 7-quart casserole or Dutch oven. When all the

49

ribs have been browned, add the onion, carrot, celery, leek and garlic to the sauté pan and brown them over medium heat. Transfer vegetables to the casserole.

Discard excess oil from the sauté pan and add red wine. Deglaze the pan over high heat, scraping the browned bits. Pour wine into the casserole, along with the chicken broth, herbs, and tomatoes. Cover with foil and cook ribs for 3 hours, basting the meat every hour. Test with a fork for doneness; the meat should be nearly falling off the bone.

Transfer the ribs to a sheet pan and reserve them in a warm place. Strain the braising liquid into a pot, discarding the cooked vegetables, and skim the surface with a ladle to remove all excess fat. Boil this liquid and reduce it to a sauce-like consistency. Adjust seasoning with salt and pepper and pour over the ribs. Serve immediately.

Serves 12

 Roll and heat damp washcloths in the microwave for 45 seconds. Pass to guests for a refreshing clean-up after a round of messy ribs.

Morning Mood: Use newspapers as trivets (with, perhaps, the *National Enquirer* at the top to start some lively conversation).

Euro Brunch

A MOMENT TO SAVOR – It is Sunday, and the world pays scant attention to the week ahead. Tomorrow is still far off, an unseen land beyond the horizon. It will appear, in due time, to spoil the view. But until then there is a deck to stretch out on, a nap to take, a reverie to slip into. Amid fresh roses and the scent of cooking eggs, welcome your guests

DAYS OF WINE AND ROSES

ON A SUNDAY MORNING

to a languid brunch, where time and people move slowly, and where nothing is required of anyone but a moderate appetite. Start by buying some pastries—croissants, Danish, scones, whatever you like—and serving them out of the box. Next, find a good baguette or two and some Nutella, a delicious chocolate and hazelnut spread from Italy. You'll be surprised at how many people indulge their chocolate obsession, even in the morning. Now you have time for the menu's centerpiece: individual fritattas (Italian open-face omelets). Although you'll put in some time at the stove, these fritattas are not difficult to make. Enlist the help of a few friends who enjoy cracking an egg or two in the morning. Serve the fritattas with prosciutto-wrapped grissini (Italian breadsticks) for an updated version of bacon and eggs. For drinks, stock up on Orangina, a wildly popular soft drink in Europe. It's not too sweet, lightly carbonated and mixes well with gin, vodka or Champagne.

ORANGINA WITH VODKA, GIN OR CHAMPAGNE
PASTRIES (IN THE BOX)
NUTELLA WITH BAGUETTES
GRISSINI WITH PROSCIUTTO
ASSORTED FRITATTA

GRISSINI WITH PROSCIUTTO

Chef's note: Grissini are Italian breadsticks from the famed Piedmont region. Here they are appropriately combined with true Italian Parma ham to make an excellent accompaniment to egg dishes or a delicious hors d'oeuvre. They can be found baked fresh at many Euro-style bakeries.

- 12 grissini
- 12 slices prosciutto di Parma

Roll prosciutto slices around the top one-third portion of each grissini. Store grissini in a cool part of the room, covered, until ready to serve.

Serves 12

ASSORTED FRITATTA

- 18 eggs
- Salt and pepper
- 8 tablespoons (1 stick) butter
- 3/4 cup freshly grated Parmesan cheese
- 3/4 cup minced chives

Splurge on roses. Buy them two days beforehand and place them in water so they have time to open.

- 4 ounces sliced smoked salmon
- 1/2 cup roasted red pepper, julienned
- 1 cup smoked shrimp
- 1 cup sautéed mushrooms, such as oyster or shiitake
- 1 cup diced sauté onions
- 5 tomatoes sliced into 1/4 inch rings

topping portions are for 3 fritattas each

Preheat the broiler. Crack the eggs into a bowl and beat them until the yolks and whites are completely incorporated and the egg no longer clings to the whisk. Season with salt and freshly cracked black pepper.

In an 8-inch nonstick skillet, melt 1 teaspoon of the butter over high heat. Add 1/4 cup of the egg mixture and tilt the pan to cover the entire bottom. Run a heat-resistant rubber scraper around the sides of the pan. Sprinkle the fritatta with 1 table-spoon of minced chives and top with a thin layer of the desired topping. Lightly sprinkle with 1 tablespoon grated Parmesan cheese and place the skillet under the broiler. Broil until the fri-tatta is lightly browned on top. Remove from the pan and serve immediately with prosciutto-wrapped grissini.

Serves 10 to 12

Party Tunes: Amuse yourself in the most classical way with Rimsky-Korsakoff's *Flight of the Bumblebee* while flipping fritattas. Or, for a more sober moment, put on Vivaldi's *Four Seasons.*

Black-eyed peas are a New Year's Day tradition in the South and are said to bring good luck.

Bayou Bash

I SEE A PARTY IN YOUR FUTURE – The cards don't lie. Face up on the table, bathed in candlelight, the tarot deck stares up and tells you the truth you already know: It's time to get some friends over and go a little crazy. And what better way than to point the compass south to Louisiana for some ice-cold beer, boiled peanuts, black-eyed peas and fondue made with crab. New Orleans is America's capital of all things weird and fun, from Anne Rice and Zydeco music to Mardi Gras beads and giant hurricane cocktails. But keep in mind that America is full of rich cultures. You can create a similar regional dinner concept for New Mexico, the Pacific Northwest, New England, the High Plains, the Gulf Coast—even Milwaukee would work (beer, brats, bowling). But for now, it's back to the Bayou. We start with some simple and fun party snacks: potato chips (we recommend Zapp's Crawtator flavor) and boiled peanuts, a fixture at roadside stands throughout the South. The feast proceeds with a black-eyed pea concoction culled from an old Junior League cookbook and a cheesy crab fondue. After some refreshments and general loosening up, move on the tarot cards, which can liven up any party. If no one knows how to read the cards, entrust the task to the most theatrical of your friends (that is, whoever can fake it the best). You may be surprised at what secrets are revealed. More than one non-believer has left the table shaking his head at the deadly accuracy of the deal. Finally, don't forget the chicory coffee to keep everyone wired.

LOOK TO AMERICA'S REGIONS
FOR PARTY INSPIRATION

DIXIE OR OTHER REGIONAL BEER
ZAPP'S POTATO CHIPS, OR OTHER KETTLE CHIPS
BLACK-EYED PEA DIP
BOILED PEANUTS
CRAB FONDUE
CHICORY COFFEE

BLACK-EYED PEA DIP

- 5 cups uncooked black-eyed peas
- 1 cup sour cream
- Juice of 2 lemons
- 2 tablespoons red pepper flakes
- 2 red bell peppers, finely diced
- 2 tomatoes, peeled, seeded, and chopped
- 1/2 cup chopped fresh parsley
- 1 cup diced country ham

Soak peas overnight. The next day, drain peas and place in a large pot. Cover with water, bring to a boil, and cook for approximately 1 hour, or until very tender. Drain and place in a large bowl. In a food processor puree 1/3 of the cooked peas and pass through a mesh strainer. Return puree to the bowl and combine with the remaining peas. Season with salt and freshly cracked black pepper. Stir in the remaining ingredients. Adjust final seasonings and serve with potato chips.

Serves 20

The origin of tarot cards is, appropriately, shrouded in mystery.
They contain imagery and symbols from many civilizations, ancient and modern.

BOILED PEANUTS

- 5 pounds raw peanuts in the shell
- 5 quarts water
- $^1/_2$ cup salt
- 1 tablespoon paprika
- 1 tablespoon cayenne pepper
- 1 tablespoon curry powder

Combine all ingredients in a stock pot. Bring to a boil and simmer for a minimum of 2 hours. If the water level falls below the peanuts, add more to cover. The peanuts are done when the shells are easy to remove and the peanuts inside are tender. Keep the peanuts in their cooking liquid until just before serving. Serve hot.

Serves 20

 All together now...pick up color-coded fondue forks at houseware stores or use bamboo skewers for communal crowd eating.

CRAB FONDUE

- 5 tablespoons butter
- 12 yellow onions, coarsely chopped
- 2 quarts unsalted chicken broth
- 1 bay leaf
- 1 sprig thyme
- Pepper
- 1/4 cup flour
- 2 red bell peppers, finely diced
- 2 green bell peppers, finely diced
- 2 red onions, finely diced
- 2 teaspoons cayenne pepper
- 1 cup heavy cream
- 1 1/2 cups diced fontina cheese
- 2 pounds crabmeat
- Salt
- 3 baguettes, cubed

In a thick-bottomed 4-quart saucepan, melt 1 tablespoon of the butter over medium heat and brown slightly. Add the chopped yellow onions and cook slowly until browned. Add the chicken broth, bay leaf, and thyme sprig. Bring mixture to a boil and reduce heat to a low simmer. Season with freshly cracked black pepper. Cover pan and braise onions for 2 hours.

Party Tunes: Spin some old pop songs from the carefree '70s, like Three Dog Night's "Mama Told Me Not to Come" or "Witchy Woman" by The Eagles.

Remove onions from braising liquid. Discard the bay leaf and thyme. Boil the broth until it is reduced to 2 cups. Puree reduced broth with the cooked onions in a blender or food processor until smooth. In the same saucepan, cleaned, melt the remaining 4 tablespoons of butter. Add the flour, stirring constantly, and cook over medium heat for 3 minutes until roux is well blended and blond in color. Add the onion puree and stir to combine. Add the red pepper, green pepper, red onion, cayenne pepper, heavy cream and diced fontina. Stir until cheese is melted, then add crabmeat. When heated through, add salt to taste. Transfer to a fondue pot and serve with cubed baguette.

Serves 20

SCATTER MARDI GRAS BEADS,
COSTUME JEWELRY, AND LOTS
OF CANDLES ON YOUR TABLE

 No tarot reading would be complete without some moody candlelight.
All you need now are a full moon and a howling wolf.

Lambic, the world's oldest type of beer, was first produced 30,000 years ago—and anthropologists believe the first brewers were women.

La Fête Belge

TRAVELERS' ADVISORY – The good people of Brussels are fond of advising travelers making the rounds of Europe to save their serious indulgences for Belgium. Here, in one small but distinguished country, is a formidable gastronomic lineup: the best chocolate, the best beer, the best mussels and the best French fries. "You can always diet in Paris,"

CAPTURE THE EASY CHARM OF A BISTRO IN BRUSSELS

Belgians say in mirthful tones, to which the only intelligent response is: "*Plus des frites, s'il vous plait.*" Fortunately, the very simplicity of Belgium's cuisine—and the growing availability of its famous beers and ales in this country—make it easy to transform your own *maison* into a charming facsimile of a bustling, happy bistro just off the Grand Place de Bruxelles. Start with the renowned lambic beer of Belgium's Payottenland. Infused with cherries, peaches or other fruits, lambics are the height of the brewer's art; many first-time tasters mistake it for Champagne or wine. Mussels are ubiquitous and cheap in Belgium. Preparing them for company (depending on the number and appetites) will likely mean cooking in batches. Sample as you finish a batch to reward yourself. As for the fries, take the easy way out. Have your friends stop at McDonald's on the way to the party. For dessert, however, bring out the real thing. Chocolate connoisseurs know that Belgian confections are the world's finest. Several kinds, including Neuhaus, Leonidas and Godiva, are widely available in the United States.

BELGIAN FRUIT BEERS, SUCH AS
MORT SUBITE PECHE, CASSIS, FRAMBOISE AND KRIEK*

MUSSELS STEAMED IN WHITE WINE
FRENCH FRIES
BELGIAN CHOCOLATE*

*see Resource Guide

MUSSELS STEAMED IN WHITE WINE

Chef's note: When purchasing mussels, look for tightly closed shells. If some are slightly open, test for liveness by tapping the hinges onto a hard surface. Discard those that do not close. To debeard, use a towel to remove fibrous material from the mussel shells. If using a wok, cook the mussels in 3 batches, dividing the wine and vegetables accordingly.

- 1/4 cup extra-virgin olive oil
- 1/2 cup finely chopped garlic
- 12 leeks, white part only, chopped
- 6 carrots, chopped
- 1 onion, chopped
- 5 celery stalks, chopped
- 8 pounds mussels, well washed, with beards removed
- 2 bottles dry white wine
- 3 cups peeled and diced tomatoes
- 1 cup chopped fresh parsley
- 3 sticks butter
- Salt and pepper

 The Manneken Pis is the beloved mascot of Brussels. The original stands proudly in the heart of the city.

In a large stockpot or wok, heat the olive oil over high heat. Add the garlic and sauté briefly without browning. Add the leeks, carrots, onion, and celery and continue to cook over high heat for 3 minutes. Add the mussels and wine and stir to combine. Cover pot and allow to cook undisturbed until you can see wisps of steam coming from the lid (about 5 minutes). Remove the lid and stir again. Add the tomatoes, parsley, and butter. Cover again and cook another 3 to 5 minutes, or until the mussels have fully opened. Discard any unopened mussels. Taste the broth and add salt and freshly cracked pepper to taste. Serve mussels in individual warm bowls, with a portion of their broth, or serve directly from the pot.

Serves 12

Nothing is quite so charming as candlelight. Wedge thin tapers into a florist's "frog." For the perfect impromptu table-cloth, ask your fish monger for extra white butcher paper when you purchase mussels.

There's a strong trend in the United States today to create authentic European-style cheeses.

Farmhouse

THE QUEST FOR QUALITY - There is something new under the sun, and it's cheese. Really exquisite cheese. Made in America. Over the last decade, America's quest for the finest native ingredients and foods has encompassed everything from organic farming to artisan bakeries to the focal point for this party—farmhouse cheeses. In rural corners from Vermont to California, a new breed of farmers is producing cheeses in small quantities, using the methods of European artisans but forging uniquely American styles and flavors. Cheese aficionados rate many of these new-wave cheeses on a par with the best of Europe. Your guests will agree. For this sampling party, we start with the mildest cheese—a Vermont quark made into a delicious, low-fat spread. Next we offer fresh mozzarella, also mild, then proceed up the strength scale through goat cheeses, Pecorino Romano and finally to the piquant and celebrated Maytag Blue. Serve strictly American wines with these cheeses, starting with lighter whites and ending with full-bodied reds.

The table setting for this sublimely rustic spread should be simple and natural. Use a backdrop of ferns or single blooms gathered from your garden and placed in individual jars and bottles. Set them on a "tablecloth" of draped gauze or muslin. Place the cheeses, breads, accompaniments and wines on plain cutting boards and straw mats to highlight the beauty of the food and drink.

DISTINCTLY AMERICAN WINES
AND FARMHOUSE CHEESES

1996 ARCHERY SUMMIT VIRETON PINOT GRIS,
RED HILLS, OREGON

1995 QUAIL RIDGE CABERNET SAUVIGNON,
NAPA VALLEY, CALIFORNIA

VERMONT QUARK CHEESE WITH SCALLIONS AND RADISH
AMERICAN FARMHOUSE CHEESES
PINEAPPLE AND GOLDEN RAISIN CHUTNEY
CRUSTY COUNTRY BREADS
SEASONAL FRUIT

VERMONT QUARK CHEESE WITH SCALLIONS AND RADISH

Chef's note: Vermont quark cheese is not technically a cheese, but a by-product of the cheesemaking process made from the whey.

- 2 cups quark cheese*
- 5 scallions, chopped
- 1 cup coarsely chopped radishes
- 2 tablespoons extra-virgin olive oil

* see Resource Guide

Combine quark, scallions, and radishes in a serving bowl. Season to taste with salt and pepper. Pour olive oil over the mixture and grate a bit more pepper over the top.

Serves 12 to 14

Surround votives with river rocks to create a fresh country ambiance.

AMERICAN FARMHOUSE CHEESES*

Chef's note: There's a strong trend in the United States today to create authentic European-style cheeses. The cheesemakers listed in the Resource Guide have been pioneers in this movement, making limited quantities of high-quality handmade cheeses. The cheeses are listed below in the preferred order of tasting.

Select 4 to 6 cheeses and purchase 1 pound of each cheese. Allow to come to room temperature before serving. With the cheeses serve simple crusty breads, fresh fruit such as grapes and apples, and Pineapple and Golden Raisin Chutney.

- Quark – use to make Vermont Quark Cheese with Scallions and Radish
- Mozzarella – use fresh mozzarella, packed in water
- Crocodile Tear – paprika-dusted, medium-aged goat cheese
- Wabash Cannonball – goat cheese rolled in ash
- Banon – goat cheese that is wrapped in a chestnut leaf and dipped in brandy and white wine
- Pecorino Romano – spicy, well-aged cheese made from sheep's milk
- Maytag Blue – creamy, piquant blue cheese aged in caves

* see Resource Guide for ordering information

Serves 12 to 14

Table Tips: Strive for simplicity with natural fabric napkins and clear glassware. Make the cheese the focus, and leave all else subdued.

PINEAPPLE AND GOLDEN RAISIN CHUTNEY

Chef's note: This chutney can be made several days ahead. In fact, it is better when the flavors have time to develop.

- 1 pineapple, peeled, cored, and coarsely chopped
- $^1/_2$ cup golden raisins
- 1 vanilla bean, split, pulp and seeds removed
- 3 apples, peeled, cored, and diced
- 1 cinnamon stick
- 1 cup sugar
- 3 cups white wine

Combine all ingredients in a stainless steel saucepan. Stir with a wooden spoon and bring to a boil. Reduce heat and simmer until nearly all the liquid is gone (about 30 to 45 minutes) and the mixture has achieved a jam-like consistency. Continue to cook, stirring constantly, until the chutney begins to stick to the bottom of the pan. Remove from heat, transfer chutney to a glass bowl, and cover the surface of the chutney directly with plastic wrap. Serve at room temperature.

Makes 2 cups

Artists' palettes make intriguing cheese spreaders and reinforce the American craftsman motif of this party.

Party Tunes: Few singers capture the sweetness—and bitter sweetness—of life like Cesaria Evora, a star in Europe and South America who sings in Portuguese and comes from Africa.

Vin Santo

RENAISSANCE DESSERT – It is late at night and all but a few of your guests have left. You sit on the patio or in the kitchen. The last, best moment of the party has arrived, and it's time for the sweet perfection of Vin Santo—the renowned "holy wine" of Tuscany. Vin Santo's grapes are harvested late, then air-dried over the winter until holy season, a process that intensely concentrates the natural sugars in the fruit. The product is a dessert wine of singular character with varying tones of honey, vanilla, chestnut and cinnamon. The region from which it hails is as sublime as the wine. Indeed, Tuscany is the cradle of the Renaissance and home to all things beautiful, from Michelangelo's David to Gucci's bags. In this shimmering land, biscotti fills a small but important niche—in this case, the cookie jar. These dry, crumbly dipping cookies have thoroughly conquered America in recent years, and they make the perfect accompaniment to the Vin Santo. Biscotti is fairly easy to make, but with so many delicious choices available in groceries, gourmet shops, coffeehouses, and neighborhood bakeries, you may wish to buy your cookies and spend your extra time on more fulfilling endeavors. Like learning a few words of Italian. Start with *amore.*

SUBMERGE YOUR GUESTS IN THE TASTES OF TUSCANY

VIN SANTO

ASSORTED BISCOTTI

VIN SANTO

Chef's note: Biscotti are twice baked Italian biscuits. Serve them with chilled Vin Santo.

- 1991 Castello di Ama
- 1991 Val D'Arbia
- 1992 Longarotti
- 1995 Brolio

BISCOTTI

Italians are fond of dipping their biscotti in their Vin Santo. Biscotti are equally wonderful dipped in steaming cups of latte. Countless varieties are available at groceries, coffeehouses and bakeries. We suggest a sampling of the more classic flavors. Offer a selection of hazelnut, almond, and fennel seed biscotti.

Allow 2 to 3 per person

A few hands of cards over a glass of port - a pastime for the ages.

Vintage Ports

THE LION IN WINTER – In the snow, in the cold, in the rhapsody of winter wind and boots crunching on ice, there is somewhere a fire to come home to. Alive with twigs and logs and yesterday's paper, the flames dance for a dozing cat and a roomful of friends. There are games and music and laughter. And there is port, itself a fire that warms, sitting properly on a sideboard. A fortified wine, port is made by adding brandy to young red wine. There are many different types of port; one could fill a book explaining the differences between ruby, tawny, late-bottled vintage, vintage and the like. The main points to note are that ports are delicious, they are all fairly sweet and most of them are an excellent value. Great ports are much cheaper than great wines. If you want the best, get vintage port. Only select years are even "declared" vintage years by the port houses, so you can't go wrong with any year you choose—a decided advantage. Port, despite its sweetness, goes surprisingly well with meals. But it's best, perhaps, with dessert. A simple dessert pairing of port with an assortment of dried fruits makes an elegant change of pace from cake and coffee. The port induces a warm and happy glow—just what you want your friends to remember as they say good night.

SPREAD SOME WARMTH
THROUGH THE WORLD

PORTS

- 1990 Grahams Malvedos, Porto
- 1997 Warres, Porto
- Founders Reserve Porto, non-vintage

DRIED FRUITS

DATES

Select medjool organic dates that are still plump and not too shriveled for a moist, sweet flavor.

FIGS

Calimyrna figs are best.

PINEAPPLE

Dried pineapple offers a lush, exotic taste.

 Party Tunes: Altan, one of the foremost traditional Irish bands, plays a blend of haunting airs and rapid, happy reels.

"Here, here have a cigar. Go on, light it up and be somebody." —an unidentified extra speaking to Jack Webb in the 1955 film *Pete Kelley's Blues.*

Cognac

AND A CIGAR ASSORTMENT

THE THIN BLUE HAZE – A scant 90 miles of blue sea separates Key West from the shores of Cuba. If there was a bridge you could leave after breakfast, arrive before lunch and be home by dinner—all with ample time for a leisurely stroll on the beach, a brief counsel with Fidel and a trip to the smoke shop. But life isn't so simple. Cuba remains a long way off, thanks to the 1962 U.S. trade embargo. Of course, enterprising Americans have long been sneaking Cohibas and other brands past customs agents after trips to Europe and Canada. And a vigorous black market exists as well. Meanwhile, law-abiding smokers turn to excellent Honduran, Dominican and Jamaican cigars. After years of decline, cigars are back in vogue. Fine restaurants offer cigar rooms. Bars and clubs are built around cigar themes. Women are a part of the craze, with many indulging for the first time and reveling in the chance to be one of the boys and infiltrate one more male dominion. What's the attraction? Is it the taste? The symbolism? Rebellion against a health-obsessed culture? Or is it simply too cool to pass up, too evocative of the nightclub good life? Someday, the answers may come. And so might those elusive Cuban cigars. Until then, smoke what you can, and what you like—the number of sizes, styles and brands is enormous (see our Resource Guide). And be content that at least there are no legal obstacles to stop you from enjoying the very best in spirits—XO Cognac from France. After all, they're only socialists. Renowned producers include Courvoisier, Hennessy, Remy-Martin, Camus and Martell. The XO designation signifies the highest quality, followed by VSOP and VS.

IT'S THE LUSH LIFE CALLING, WITH COGNAC AND CIGARS

COGNAC

- Courvoisier XO
- Hennessey VSOP
- Camus Napoléon XO

CIGARS

MILD BODIED –
- La Unica
- Macanudo
- Dunhill (Dominican)

MEDIUM BODIED –
- Davidoff 1000 Series
- Montecristo
- Romeo y Julieta

FULL BODIED –
- Arturo Fuente (Chateau & Hemingway Series)
- Avo Uvezian
- PG/ Paul Garmirian Gourmet Series

 A cigar cutter is essential—and so, some would say, are the Altoid peppermints.

ABC Carpet & Home
888 Broadway
New York, NY 10003
212/473-3000
(glassware, dinnerware, linens, fabrics, housewares)

A.L. Bazzini
339 Greenwich Street
New York, NY 10013
212/334-1280
(dried fruits, nuts, chocolates)

Ad Hoc Softwares
410 West Broadway
New York, NY 10012
212/925-2652
(glassware, dinnerware, linens)

Antique Addiction
436 West Broadway
New York, NY 10012
212/925-6342
(vintage glassware, dinnerware)

Anthropologie
375 West Broadway
New York, NY 10012
212/343-7070
215/564-2313 (for additional store locations)
(glassware, dinnerware, linens)

Aphrodisia
264 Bleeker Street
New York, NY 10014
212/989-6440
(dried herbs)

Banana Republic
2 Harrison Street
San Francisco, CA 94105
415/777-0250
(glassware, dinnerware, linens)

Barney's New York
660 Madison Avenue
New York, NY 10021
212/826-8900
800/822-7639 (for additional store locations)
(glassware, dinnerware, linens)

Bella Cucina Artful Food
800/580-5674 (for catalogue)
(gourmet foods, kitchenware)

Bridge Kitchenware
214 East 52 Street
New York, NY 10022
212/838-6746
(kitchenware)

Broadway Panhandler
477 Broome Street
New York, NY 10022
212/966-3434
(kitchenware)

Calvin Klein Home
800/294-7978 (for nearest retailer)
(glassware, dinnerware, linens)

Capriole, Inc.
PO Box 117
Greenville, IN 47124
To order: 504/558-9992
*(farmhouse cheeses including
Wabash Canonball, Banon, Crocodile Tear)*

Caribou Coffee Company
800/576-3412 (for store locations)
888/CARIBOU (for catalogue)
www.caribou-coffee.com
(gourmet coffees, teas, accessories)

C'est Moi
3198 Paces Ferry Place
Atlanta, GA 30305
404/467-0095
(glassware, dinnerware, ceramics, linens)

Chef
1046 North Highland Avenue
Atlanta, GA 30306
404/875-2433
(kitchenware)

Collage
800/9-COLLAGE (for catalogue)
www.flaxart.com
(fine papers, gifts)

Crate & Barrel
800/451-8217 (for store locations)
800/323-5461 (for catalogue)
(housewares, kitchenware)

D'Artagnan
800/327-8246
www.ippi.com/dartagnan.html
(foie gras, gourmet foods)

Dean & Deluca
800/221-7714 (for catalogue)
www.dean-deluca.com
(gourmet foods, kitchenware)

DOM (USA), Inc.
693 Fifth Avenue
New York, NY 10012
212/334-5580
(housewares, kitchenware)

Felissimo
10 West 56th Street
New York, NY 10019
212/247-5656
(glassware, dinnerware, linens)

Ferrara
195 Grand Street
New York, NY 10013
800/533-6910
www.ferraracafe.com
(biscotti, pastries)

Fillamento
2185 Fillmore Street
San Francisco, CA 94115
415/931-6304
(glassware, dinnerware, linens)

Global Beer Network
805/967-8111
www.globalbeer.com
(Belgian fruit beers)

Godiva
800/9-GODIVA (for store locations)
www.godiva.com
(Belgian chocolates)

Hancock Fabrics
601/842-2834 (for store locations)
www.fabric1.com
(fabrics, sewing accessories)

Holt's Cigar Company
2270 Townsend Road
Philadelphia, PA 19154
800/523-1641
www.holts.com
(fine cigars)

Homesick Gourmet
http://homesickgourmet.radish.net/
(regional specialty foods)

IKEA
908/289-4488 (for West Coast store locations)
412/747-0747 (for East Coast store locations)
(housewares)

Indian Harvest Specialty Foods
800/294-2433 (for catalogue)
www.indianharvest.com
(purple Thai rice)

Internet Antique Shop
800/294-2433 (for catalogue)
www.tias.com
(antiques, collectibles)

Kate's Paperie
561 Broadway
New York, NY 10012
800/809-9880 (for catalogue)
(fine paper, gifts)

Kelley and Ping
127 Greene Street
New York, NY 10012
212/228-1212
(Asian foods)

Le Creuset of America, Inc.
800/827-1798
(cookware)

Lemon Grass
367 West Broadway
New York, NY 10013
212/343-0900
(candles)

La Paysanne Pecorino
Route 3, PO Box 27
Hayward, MN 56043
507/256-4788
(farmhouse cheeses including Pecorino Romano)

Leonidas
485 Madison Avenue
New York, NY 10012
212/980-2608
(Belgian chocolates)

Logan Turnpike Mill
3485 Gainesville Highway
Blairsville, GA 30512
800/84-GRITS
(stone-ground grits)

Maytag Dairy Farms
PO Box 806
Newton, IA 50208
800/247-2458
(farmhouse cheeses including Maytag Blue)

Metropolitan Deluxe
1034 Highland Avenue
Atlanta, GA 30306
404/892-9337
(candles, glassware, dinnerware, linens)

The MOMA Design Store
800/447-MOMA (for catalogue)
44 West 53rd Street
New York, NY 10019
212/767-1050
www.moma.org/stores.html
(housewares, glassware, dinnerware)

Mood Indigo
181 Prince Street
New York, NY 10012
212/254-1176
(vintage glassware, dinnerware)

Moss
146 Greene Street
New York, NY 10012
212/226-2190
(20th century industrial design products)

The Mozzarella Company
2944 Elm Street
Dallas, TX 75226
800/798-2954
(assorted cheeses including mozzarella)

Mr. Tequila's Cantina
http://users.aol.com/mrtequila/home.htm
(guide to tequila)

Neuhaus Chocolates
9229 Madison Avenue
New York, NY 10021
212/861-2800
(Belgian chocolates)

Open Air Markets

www.openair.org

(guide to street markets, flea markets, farmer's markets)

Pariscope

http://pariscope.fr

(Paris shopping, antiques, flea markets)

Pier 1 Imports, Inc.

800/245-4595 (for store locations)

www.pier1.com

(housewares, kitchenware)

Pottery Barn

800/922-5507 (for catalogue)

800/922-9934 (for store locations)

www.dreamshop.com

(housewares, kitchenware)

Provenance

1155 Foster Street

Atlanta, GA 30318

404/351-1217

(antiques, collectibles, dinnerware, linens)

Restoration Hardware

415/924-1005 (for store locations)

www.restorationhardware.com

(housewares)

Sam Flax, Inc.

1460 Northside Drive

Atlanta, GA 30318

404/352-7200

425 Park Avenue

New York, NY 10016

212/620-3060

12 West 20th Street

New York, NY 10011

212/620-3038

(art supplies)

Seattle's Best Coffee

800/962-9659 (for catalogue)

800/722-3190 (for store locations)

www.seabest.com

(gourmet coffees, accessories)

Seeds of Change

888/762-4240

www.seedsofchange.com

(organic seeds, organic foods)

Starbucks Coffee

800/782-7282 (for catalogue)

800/447-1575 (for store locations)

www.starbucks.com

(gourmet coffees, accessories)

Takashimaya, Inc.

693 Fifth Avenue

New York, NY 10012

800/753-2038 (for catalogue)

(Japanese glassware, dinnerware, linens)

Target Stores

612/304-6073 (call collect for store locations)

www.targetstores.com

(housewares, kitchenware)

Tinder Box

888/827-0947 (for catalogue and store locations)

www.tinderbox.com

(fine tobacco products)

Tribeca Potters

443 Greenwich Street

New York, NY 10013

212/431-7631

(custom pottery)

Uproar

121 Greene Street

New York, NY 10012

212/614-8580

203/221-9230

(glassware, dinnerware, linens)

Versace Fifth Avenue

647 Fifth Avenue, 5th floor

New York, NY 10022

212/317-0224

212/582-3473 (for additional store locations)

(glassware, dinnerware, linens)

Vermont Butter and Cheese Company

Pitman Road, PO Box 95

Websterville, VT 05678

800/884-6287

(farmhouse cheeses including quark)

World Variety Produce, Inc.

PO Box 21127

Los Angeles, CA 90021

800/588-0151

www.melissa.com

(dried fruits, grains, nuts)

Williams-Sonoma

800/541-2233 (for catalogue)

800/541-1262 (for store locations)

www.williams-sonoma.com

(glassware, cookware, dinnerware, linens)

Wolfman-Gold & Good Company
117 Mercer Street
New York, NY 10012
212/966-8268
(glassware, dinnerware, linens)

Zabar's
2245 Broadway
New York, NY 10024
212/787-2000
800/697-6301 (for catalogue)
(gourmet foods)

Zapp's Potato Chips
PO Box 1533
Gramercy, LA 70052
800/HOTCHIP
www.zapps.com
(potato chips)

Zona
97 Greene Street
New York, NY 10012
212/925-6750
(glassware, dinnerware, linens)

Add your name to the Modern mailing list! - call/fax - 770/594-0099

ACKNOWLEDGMENTS

Many thanks to Shaun Doty, the executive chef at Mumbo Jumbo, for sharing his brilliant culinary talent with me. The opportunity to work with this enthusiastic and talented chef has been a highlight of my career. I also want to thank Paul Sullivan of Mumbo Jumbo for his constant attention to detail, insight into the latest restaurant/club trends and ability to make things happen. And thank you to their colleagues, Oscar Morales and Chris Calhoun. To Vivian Mize, designer extraordinaire and my touchstone, many thanks. Thanks to the talented Matthew De Galan for helping make sense out of a mountain of information. I want to thank Brad Newton for capturing the vibrant images on these pages. Thank you to my very chic editor, Suzanne De Galan, for truly valuable input. Thanks to my agent, Stedman Mays, with whom I have the tightest Internet connection possible. To my sister, Sheila, and her husband, Ron, who are embarking on a new life together, congratulations! To my husband, Doug Sandberg, a key part of the *Modern* team, I love you. This party book is fittingly dedicated to the late Jacquie Gatling, a vibrant, young woman who loved life, parties and wearing her hair in countless styles and colors. I am grateful to have had the good fortune to work closely with her. Jacquie, I thought I had so much to teach you, but you have been and will always be my teacher. Peace. And lastly to my children, Charley and Caroline, follow your hearts and celebrate this party called life.